SERMON OUTLINES

ON THE

FRUIT

OF THE

SPIRIT

Books by Al Bryant

Climbing the Heights
Day by Day with C. H. Spurgeon
More Sermon Outlines for Special Occasions
More Sermon Outlines on Prayer
New Every Morning
Revival Sermon Outlines
Sermon Outlines for Evangelistic Occasions
Sermon Outlines for Funerals and Other Special Occasions
Sermon Outlines for Lay Leaders
Sermon Outlines on Bible Characters (Old Testament)
Sermon Outlines on Bible Characters (New Testament)
Sermon Outlines on the Attributes of God
Sermon Outlines on the Cross of Christ
Sermon Outlines on the Deeper Life
Sermon Outlines on Faith, Hope, and Love
Sermon Outlines on Family and Home
Sermon Outlines on the Fruit of the Spirit
Sermon Outlines on the Grace of God
Sermon Outlines on the Life of Christ
Sermon Outlines on Prayer
Sermon Outlines on Prophetic Themes
Sermon Outlines for Special Occasions
Sermon Outlines for Worship Services
Sourcebook of Poetry

SERMON OUTLINES

ON THE

FRUIT

OF THE

SPIRIT

compiled by
Al Bryant

PUBLICATIONS

Grand Rapids, MI 49501

Sermon Outlines on the Fruit of the Spirit by Al Bryant

Copyright © 1996 by Kregel Publications, a division of Kregel, Inc., P.O. Box 2607, Grand Rapids, MI 49501. Kregel Publications provides trusted, biblical publications for Christian growth and service. Your comments and suggestions are valued.

Cover and book design: Alan G. Hartman

Library of Congress Cataloging-in-Publication Data
Bryant, Al (1926–
    Sermon outlines on the fruit of the Spirit / [compiled by] Al Bryant.
        p.   cm.
    1. Fruit of the Spirit—Sermons—Outlines, syllabi, etc.
I. Bryant, Al, 1926–
BT122.S47   1996   251'.02—dc20   96-30472
                                                 CIP

ISBN 0-8254-2155-1

Printed in the United States of America
1 2 3 4 5 / 00 99 98 97 96

CONTENTS

PREFACE

It is interesting to note the apostle Paul's emphasis on love in his New Testament writings, and also the apostle John's frequent reference to the same subject. But throughout the Scriptures love is the very nature of God. If He could be summed up in a word, it would be that word *love* (in John 4:8 the apostle says, "God is love").

So it should not be surprising that in his list of the fruits of the Spirit, Paul begins with love and goes on to list eight other "fruits," none of which could exist without love at the center. And in 1 Corinthians 13 he lauds love as the greatest spiritual gift of all (v. 13). That is why outlines on love (our love for God and His for us) dominate this book.

You will note that the outlines in this collection have been grouped under several heads, beginning with love, but the idea of love rises up throughout the whole book, just as it should rise up in our lives as Christians. I have also added suitable poems* and illustrations throughout the compilation to enhance the message of these timeless outlines. May this compilation enrich your preaching and teaching.

AL BRYANT

* The poems in this compilation are used by permission and taken from *Sourcebook of Poetry* published in 1992 by Kregel Publications.

SCRIPTURE INDEX

INTENSITY OF LOVE

Set me as a seal upon thine heart, as a seal upon thine arm: for love is strong as death. . . . Many waters cannot quench love, neither can the floods drown it (Song of Sol. 8:6–7).

Of this gorgeous allegory the text is one of the brightest gems. It is the fervent address of the Bride—the Church, to her beloved royal Bridegroom, and the love of God is ever to have the supremacy of all affection. The love of Christ is to have the preeminency. Jesus is God's incarnate love—the love of God is preeminently manifested in the gift and person of His Son, who became the evidence as well as the fullness of the love of God toward us.

Observe,

I. The Ardent Desire of the Church (v. 6).

"Set me as a seal," etc. It is a request to have

A. A *deep place* in His *loving heart*. Engraven within—permanently within—and abiding in His heart's love.

B. A *visible place* in His *offices* and *work*. "A seal on those without." The Church—the world—an interest in His arm's support and defense, etc. "Who is this leaning," etc. In one word, to be identified with His love and work.

II. The Grounds on Which This Desire Is Pleaded.

A. The *intensity* of *love*. "Strong as death." Now this is true

  1. Of love to Christ. Highest—deepest—most constraining of all the affections; giving impassioned desire—vehement devotion—ever present realization. But the uttermost consecration of life, labor, toils—death itself. So the apostles lived and died martyrs. But see how still more true

  2. Of Christ's love to us. The whole being of the Savior given for us. Unparalleled condescension—the deepest abasement—the extremest sufferings—the most ignominious death—"even the death of the cross." First from Christ to us—second from Christ in us—and then, third, from us to Christ. But we are led

III. To Contemplate This Marvelous Love.

In its extraordinary attributes,

A. It is *inexorable* as the *grave*. Jealous of rivalry—of opposition—to the enemies of the object beloved; and then zealous in prosecuting the designs of the Savior loved. As the grave insatiable—as the grave knowing no distinction. See it in Paul's utterance—"if any man love," etc. No matter whom, enemy or friend—alien or kindred—let the anathema rest, even on angels, etc. (Gal. 1:8).

B. In its *vehemency*. "Coals of fire"—a flame of God—fire of heaven—sacred, pure, celestial—not cold, calculating, formal.

C. Its *inextinguishableness*. "Many waters," etc. Adversity, trials, afflictions, prisons, believers drowned for Christ.

D. No *price* adequately can be *given* for it. Honors, offices, treasures, etc.

Application

Do we possess it?

Does it absorb us?

Do we evidence it?

Learn its Divine source and its eternal sacred influence, power, and preciousness.

Jabez Burns

LOVE QUESTIONED AND VINDICATED

I have loved you, says the Lord. Yet you say, wherein have you loved us?
(Mal. 1:2).

I. God's Love Declared. "I have loved you, says the Lord."

To every believer this love has been shown in—

A. Election in Christ Jesus from of old.

B. Pardon of sin, justification by faith, adoption, sanctification, etc.

C. Preservation to this hour, and promise for all future time.

This is a short list of the ways by which the Lord has said to each regenerate soul, "I have loved you."

II. God's Love Questioned. "Yet you say, Wherein have you loved us?"

Such a question has been asked—

A. Under great afflictions in which there seemed no relief. Petulantly the sorrowing one has questioned divine love.

B. In sight of the prosperous wicked in their day of pride many a poor despised believer has rashly doubted the special love of God.

C. In times of grievous doubt as to one's personal salvation, and, under heavy temptations of Satan, the same doubt has arisen.

III. God's Love Considered.

A. Love lamenting. Is God to be thus treated? Shall He mournfully cry, "I have loved you? Yet you say, Wherein have you loved us?"

B. Love entreating. Does not each accent say, "Return to Me"?

C. Love abounding. Our question shames us. God loves us in ten thousand ways; loves us so as to be patient even when we wickedly question His love.

If it would be marvelous to see one river leap up from the earth fullgrown what would it be to gaze upon a vast spring from which all the rivers of the earth should at once come bubbling up, a thousand of them born at a birth? What a vision would it be! Who can conceive it? And yet the love of God is that fountain, from which all the rivers of mercy, which have ever gladdened our race—all the rivers of grace in time, and of glory hereafter—take their rise. O my soul, stand at that sacred fountain head, and adore and magnify forever and ever God, even our Father, who has loved us.

C. H. Spurgeon

THE ELEVENTH COMMANDMENT

A new commandment I give unto you, That ye love one another, as I have loved you, that ye also love one another (John 13:34).

These words of Jesus have been fitly styled the eleventh commandment. Christ Himself calls it a new commandment. Yet not essentially, for the second great commandment was in this direction—"And thou shalt love thy neighbor as thyself," etc. But the whole text strikingly illustrates the idea of "new," when it is added,

"As I have loved you." Now in this wide and deep sense, it is indeed new. But look

I. At the Commandment Itself.

"Love one another." Now "love" includes commiseration, compassion, goodness, sympathy, benevolence, beneficence, etc. Good feeling toward others—good doing, etc. See, it is unlike

A. Isolation, or separateness.

B. Selfishness and indifference.

C. Hate and animosity.

D. Envy and uncharitableness. As in the text, it includes approbation, complacency, oneness, and kind feeling, etc. Now Paul describes it in 1 Corinthians 13. Read its items, and see its counterfeits—alms-giving, self-emulation, extraordinary gifts, etc.

Observe

II. The Model on Which It Is to Be Constructed.

"As I have," etc. Notice

A. Like Christ's, it *must* be *first*. Before they love us, or at least before they manifest it. Also it

B. May be *undeserved*. Christ loved before they were worthy, yes, in one sense, they never had a worthiness He had not given.

C. It must be *most free*. Like Christ's. Not extorted. Like the stream or the air, light, etc.

D. It must be *self-sacrificing*. Like Christ's. How Christ's love brought Him to the earth. Incarnate—abased—suffering—died, etc.

E. It must, like Christ's, be *practical* in its *results*. Bearing blessings—conveying mercies—bestowing gifts.

F. It must, like Christ's, be *lowly*. Not pompous—vain—glorious—ostentatious.

G. To all Christ's *disciples*. Each and every one.

H. It must be *abiding*, like Christ's. Having loved His own, He loved them to the end. Now see

III. The Appropriateness of the Designation.

"A new commandment," etc.

A. It is the commandment of the *new dispensation*.

B. Invested with *new authority*. "I" give unto you. He is our Lord, our Divine Head and Master.

C. It is *identified* with *new illustrations*. Moses and the prophets loved God and the church, but not as Jesus. In Him it lived supreme. His breath, words, deeds, life, death.

D. It is *supplied* with *new resources*. How are we to exemplify it? By Christ's grace—by the Spirit's work in the soul.

E. It is to be the *distinguishing feature* of the *new* kingdom. The sign—the motto—the badge—the glory! Not a kingdom of ceremonial sacrifices, but of love. Love is the essence, substance, and ground of Christianity.

Application

1. Christ's disciples are bound by this commandment.

2. For it there is no substitute.

3. In it is the perfection of blessedness. Thus we are one with God, and the Lord Jesus Christ, by His Holy Spirit dwelling in us.

Jabez Burns

LOVE'S IMPORTANCE

Ye have hard how I said unto you, I go away, and come again unto you. If ye loved Me, ye would rejoice, because I said, I go unto the Father: for My Father is greater than I" (John 14:28).

I. We Should Try to See Things in Christ's Light.

A. He sees the whole of things. He says not only, "I go away," but also, "I come again unto you."

B. He sees through things, He does not say, "I die," but He looks beyond, and says, "I go unto the Father."

C. He sees the true bearing of things. The events which were about to happen were in themselves sad, but they would lead to happy results. "If ye loved Me, ye would rejoice."

II. Our Love Should Go Forth Toward His Person.

A. He is the source of all the benefits He bestows.

B. Loving Him, we have Him, and so His benefits.

C. Loving Him, we prize His benefits the more.

D. Loving Him, we sympathize in all that He does.

E. Loving Him, we love His people for His sake.

F. Loving Him, our love endures all sorts of rejections for His sake.

G. Loving Him, the Father loves us (John 14:23).

III. Our Sorrow Ought Not to Put Our Love in Question.

Yet, in the case of the disciples, our Lord justly said, "*If* ye loved Me."

He might sorrowfully say the same to us—

A. When we complain at His will, because of our severe afflictions.

B. When we fear to die, and thus display an unwillingness to be with our Lord. Surely, if we loved Him, we should rejoice to be with Him.

IV. Our Love Should Make Us Rejoice at Our Lord's Exaltation Though It Be Our Personal Loss.

A. It was apparently the disciples' loss for their Lord to go to the Father; and we may think certain dispensations to be our loss:

When we are afflicted, and He is glorified, by our sorrows.

When we are eclipsed, and in the result the gospel is spread.

When we are deprived of privileges for the good of others.

B. It was greatly to our Lord's gain to go to His Father.

Thus He left the field of suffering forever.

Thus He reassumed the glory which He had laid aside.

Thus He received the glory awarded by the Father.

A saint cares not how ill it goes with him so it goes well with Jesus Christ; he says, as Mephibosheth to David, "Yea, let him take all, forasmuch as my lord the king is come again in peace unto his own house" (2 Sam. 19:30). So it may go well with God's name. Moses cares not though his name be blotted out of the book of life. John the Baptist said, "He must increase, but I must decrease."

—RALPH VENNING

C. H. Spurgeon

CHRISTIAN LOVE

Love one another with a pure heart fervently (1 Peter 1:22).

The love of the brethren is the test of our Christianity, and the badge of our Christian profession. It is even the essential of the new man. Without it, all religious profession is mere glitter—an empty show—a noisy cymbal. But what is this love? Let us see:

I. Its Nature.

It is admiration. Estimation and complete complacency in the Lord's people. It recognizes them as brethren and sisters in Christ, and fellow heirs of the grace of life. It will include attachment, fellowship, communion, and spiritual adhesion, and unselfish conduct and conversation.

II. Its Extent.

All the Lord's people. It is not to be sectarian, denominational, local. It is not to be limited to persons of our order, creed, or mode of worship. Every saint of God—every disciple of Jesus—every saint walking in holiness.

III. Its Special Traits.

A. It is to be the *love* of the *heart*. All else is tinsel and make-believe.

B. It is to be the love of a *pure* heart. Not love of their person, with a fleshly attachment, but love pure as light, and sanctifying as flame.

C. It is to be *hot* and *intense*. "Fervently." Not coldly—not formally—not pretentiously—not confined to the tongue, but a holy flame, fervent. Not to be quenched—not to go out, but to burn and shine in loving words and deeds—always to the glory of God.

Jabez Burns

LIFE PROVED BY LOVE

We know that we have passed from death unto life, because we love the brethren (1 John 3:14).

I. We Know That We Were Dead.
A. We were without feeling when law and gospel were addressing us.

B. Without hunger and thirst after righteousness.

C. Without power of movement toward God in repentance.

D. Without the breath of prayer, or the pulse of desire.

II. We Know That We Have Undergone a Singular Change.
A. The reverse of the natural change from life to death.

B. No more easy to describe than the death change would be.

C. This change varies in each case as to its outward manifestation, but it is essentially the same in all.

D. As a general rule its course is as follows—

It commences with painful sensations.

It leads to a sad discovery of our natural weakness.

It is made manifest by personal faith in Jesus.

It operates on the man by repentance and purification.

It is continued by perseverance in sanctification.

It is completed in joy, infinite, eternal.

E. The period of this change is an era to be looked back upon in time and through eternity with grateful praise.

III. We Know That We Live.
A. We know that faith has given us new senses, grasping a new world, enjoying a realm of spiritual things.

B. We know that we have new hopes, fears, desires, delights.

C. We know that we have new needs; such as heavenly breath, food, instruction, correction, etc.

IV. We Know That We Live, Because We Love. "We love the brethren."
A. We love them for Christ's sake.

B. We love them for the truth's sake.

C. We love them for their own sake.

D. We love them when the world hates them.

E. We love their company, their example, their exhortations.

F. We love them despite the drawbacks of infirmity, inferiority, etc.

Just as in the gospel he rescues the word *logos* from anti-Christian uses, so in this Epistle he rescues the word *know* and aims at making his "little children" Gnostics in the divine sense. Knowledge is excellent, but the path to it is not through intellectual speculation, however keen and subtle, but through faith in Jesus Christ and subjection to Him, according to those most Johannine words in the Gospel of Matthew: "Neither knoweth any man the Father save the Son, and He to whomsoever the Son will reveal Him."—CULROSS

The world always loves to believe that it is impossible to know that we are converted. If you ask them, they will say, "I am not sure; I cannot tell"; but the whole Bible declares we may receive, and know that we have received, the forgiveness of sins.   —R. M. McCHEYNE

In the early days of Christianity, when it triumphed over the old heathenism of the Roman world, it founded a new society bound together by this holy mutual love. The catacombs of Rome bear remarkable testimony to this gracious brotherhood. There were laid the bodies of members of the highest Roman aristocracy, some even of the family of the Caesars, side by side with the remains of obscure slaves and laborers.

And in the case of the earliest graves the inscriptions are without single allusion to the position in society of him who was buried there: they did not trouble themselves whether he had been a consul or a slave, a tribune of the legion or a common soldier, a patrician or an artisan. It sufficed that they knew him to have been a believer in Christ, a man who feared God. They cared not to perpetuate in death the vain distinctions of the world; they had mastered the glorious teaching of the Lord, "One is your master, even Christ, and all ye are brethren."   —E. DE PRESSENSE

C. H. Spurgeon

LOVE OF CHRIST, AND OUR LOVE TO HIM

We love him, because he first loved us (1 John 4:19).

The theme of John's epistle is love. The love of God to us. The love of Jesus as the Savior. The love of saints to the Father and His Son. The love of believers to one another. The text leads us to the love of Christ and His people.

Observe,

I.   Christ Is the Fountain of Love.

"He" first loved us. This is the universal and unvarying testimony of the Scriptures. Observe

A. The *gradations* of Christ's *love* to us.
1. In His willingness to be our Mediator. Lo I "come." Not compelled. As Isaac, by faith, was ready, etc. He desired it—sought it.
2. In the assumption of our nature. Hence the Son of man. Made of a woman. Seed of Abraham—Tribe of Judah—lineage of David. But this step was wondrous. Not the nature of angels, but lower, etc. Not man—royalty—splendor—or sacerdotal—Priest. No! He made Himself of no reputation. Bethlehem—manger—poor.
3. In taking the place of the substitute. Surety— Daysman—under law—suffering—soul sorrow— condemnation—death. "Bore our sorrows, griefs." Died the just for the unjust, etc. Sword, etc.

B. The *peculiarities* of His love.
1. Love to the base and the defiled—rebels, etc.
2. Love unsought arising out of itself. For love's sake.
3. Unparalleled. Nothing like it.
4. Infinite and inconceivable. Passing knowledge.

Notice:

II.   In and From Us Love to Christ Is Asserted.

"We love Him." This signifies, we esteem—admire—delight, and are grateful to Jesus. Heart full of Him. Now where this love is:

A. It is *real* and *sincere*. Not imaginative—not rhapsody— impulse, etc.

B. It is *conscious*. "We love Him." Know it—feel it.

C. It is *evident*. Its influence is seen, for we love His word, sanctuary, ordinances, day, people, commandments.

D. Supreme. Highest—more than father or mother, etc. Look—

III. At the Connection Between the Two.
"We," "because," etc.

A. The love flowed from Him first.

B. Manifested to us.

C. Realized by us.

D. Then returned. As rivers to the ocean—light—magnet.

E. Sustained.

Application
First, who can utter the text. *Second*, let all seek to feel it.

Jabez Burns

When I Think of His Love

When I think of the cross where my Savior died,
   'Neath the frown of the darkened skies,
When I hear the groan of the Crucified,
   And I look on those death-closed eyes,
When I know that for me He the anguish bore,
   From sin He might set me free,
Oh, I know that I'll love Him forevermore,
   When I think of His love for me.

When I think of the grave where they laid my Lord,
   And they sealed Him within the gloom,
When I think how according to His Word,
   He arose from that vanquished tomb,
Oh, I know that for me He endured it all,
   My eyes with tears grow dim,
While low at His feet in love I fall,
   Whenever I think of Him.

—Louis Paul Lehman Jr.

LOVE OF THE BROTHER
ESSENTIALLY ALLIED WITH LOVE OF GOD

That he who loveth God loves his brother also (1 John 4:21).

Love is the essence of all acceptable religion. But it must embody both aspects—love to God and love to man. Either department only presents one division of heaven-born piety.

Notice,

I.   The Love of God Must Be First and Paramount.

Here religion begins. Carnal mind renewed. Rebellious heart changed. God's love winning back the rebel—the enemy. The soul subdued, melted, inflamed with God's love—shed abroad in the heart, etc. The process is by the gospel, and the power of the gracious Spirit. This love of God will be conscious, supreme. Delighting in God and doing His holy will. It must be first in priority. First in intensity—first in its manifest fruits and evidences.

II.   The Love of Our Brother Will Ever Accompany Our Love to God.

"Love his brother also."

Notice, that this love of the brother is:

A.   The same affection in its human direction.

It does not possess some of those sublime elements that love to God does: as adoring gratefulness—absolute supremacy, but in its nature and essence, it is the one burning, sacred affection of the soul.

B.   It will give *undeniable evidences* of its *existence*.

The tongue will speak out this love. The life will exhibit it. All kind help will reveal it. It will be gracious, tender, self-denying, and self-sacrificing.

C.   Its *fruit* will be more *observable*.

Its acts and outgoings will be open to all. "So that by this all men shall know that you love one another."

D.   It will *grow* in its *vital power*, as *our love* to God *increases*.

The more we love God, the more we shall love our brother.

Application

1.   The subject is a fit test of our real Christianity.
2.   Should be assiduously cherished and cultivated.

3. Exhibited to all the brethren. The disciples of Jesus.

4. These are two essential links of the golden chain of salvation.

Jabez Burns

THE TWO ESSENTIAL LINKS

In truth and love (2 John 3).

In the first verse, the apostle speaks of the elect lady and her children, and adds, "whom I love in the truth." Now let us look,

I. At the Link Named First.

That is, "Truth." It may signify:

A. A knowledge of Divine truth, as given in Holy Scripture; or

B. A reception of evangelical truth, in its saving efficacy; or

C. The power of truth, in delivering the mind from error and superstition and sin. Giving liberty, etc. "Ye shall know the truth," etc.; or

D. Fidelity to truth—by speaking it, and professing it, and being under its practical influence; or

E. Rejoicing in the truth of the divine faithfulness, and being witnesses for it.

II. The Second Link Is Love.

A. True love to the Divine Tri-unity—Father, Son, and Holy Spirit.

B. Unfeigned love of the brethren in Christ.

C. The sympathy of compassionate love for all mankind; or,

D. Love of Divine truth, as exhibited in the Gospel system—doctrines, ordinances, profession of Christ. Having loving communion and companionship with the disciples of truth.

1. Now both of these are links of the same heavenly chain.
2. Truth must be received before divine love is experienced.
3. We believe the truth, and then love. Faith works by love.
4. They are ever to be found connected with each

other. Truth can only thrive in the atmosphere of love. And love is mere natural emotion, unless living in the vital air of truth.

5. Both indispensable in the realization of true religion.
6. The union of the two will flourish in eternal harmony and oneness.
7. Sin is falsehood and enmity; religion, truth and love. As two flowers, they grow side by side in the garden of Holy Scripture. They constitute the essentials of the gospel, and dwell in the hearts of all the children of God.

Jabez Burns

Love Wins the Day

Many lonely sailors have been cheered by the flashing signal from Minot's light off Scituate, Massachusetts. The signal spells "I love you" in nautical code. Several years ago the Coast Guard decided to replace the old equipment. They announced that for technical reasons the new machines would be unable to flash the "I love you" message. The public protested, and the Coast Guard weakened. The old equipment remains and continues to send its message of cheer to sailors.

Love Over Will Power

Aleida Juissen, 78, of Rotterdam, Netherlands, has been smoking for 50 years. And for 50 years she has been trying to give up her harmful habit. But she has not been successful—that is, until recently. She has now given up cigarettes, cigars, and pipes. The secret? Leo Jansen, 79, proposed marriage last year, but refused to go through with the wedding until Aleida gave up smoking. Says Aleida now: "Will power never was enough to get me off the tobacco habit. Love did it."

—Prairie Overcomer

THE CHRISTIAN WORKER'S DISCOURAGEMENT AND SUCCESS

He that goeth forth and weepeth, bearing precious seed, shall doubtless come again with rejoicing, bringing his sheaves with him (Ps. 126:6).

I. The Laborer.

A. The Christian worker may be compared to a sower because their office demands active exertion, because their office is important, because their office has reference to futurity.

B. The seed they scatter is precious on account of its nature, its rarity, its value, its effects.

II. Their Discouragement: "And weepeth."

A. Discouragement from a sense of their own weakness and insufficiency.

B. From the magnitude of the obstacles they encounter.

C. From the disappointment they undergo—their frequency, their distress.

D. From the sense of responsibility.

III. Their Success: "Doubtless come again with rejoicing, bringing his sheaves with him."

A. It is future.

B. It is certain.

C. It is joyful.

Selected

JOY IN BELIEVING

Now the God of hope fill you with all joy and peace in believing
(Rom. 15:13).

I. Joy and Peace Are the Inspirers of Hope.

The God of hope is he who imparts hope by the peace of God and the joy of the Lord. Joy is like the rolling waves of the sea in majesty and power; peace is like a river in its placid tranquillity. The one is love in motion; the other, love in repose. Faith and hope, like the fleecy clouds, rise above these waters to the very heavens of attainment.

Mark Guy Pearse says, "The great sea one day looked up at a pure, fleecy cloud in the very bosom of the heavens. The sea, sighing, said: 'It is not for me; I could never be like that. But I will try.' And she hurled herself against the rocks, leaping up in tall spray which fell back, baffled and beaten. At last the sea lay quiet and still, and cried out to the sun, 'Canst thou not help me?' 'Yes, I can,' said the sun, 'if thou wilt let me.' And the sun sent down a noiseless ray, warming and loosening the water; and lo! the sea knew not how, but cried, 'I am there.'"

II. Believing Is Looking Up at the Sun of Righteousness When All Our Struggles Are Over.

It is letting Him shine down upon us and lift us up into His bosom.

III. The Watchword of Our Faith of Science and Discovery Should Be, "I believe more than I see or know."

This is the victory that overcomes the world of sin, of ignorance and of undiscovered countries; faith in the unseen is the mighty revealer.

Selected

JOY A DUTY

Rejoice in the Lord always: and again I say, rejoice (Phil. 4:4).

I. The Grace Commanded. "Rejoice."

A. It is delightful; our soul's jubilee has come when joy enters.

B. It is demonstrative: it is more than peace; it sparkles, shines, sings. Why should it not? Joy is a bird; let it fly in the open heavens, and let its music be heard of all men.

C. It is stimulating, and urges its possessor to brave deeds.

D. It is influential for good. Sinners are attracted to Jesus by the joy of saints. More flies are caught with a spoonful of honey than a barrel of vinegar

E. It is contagious. Others are gladdened by our rejoicing.

F. It is commanded:

Because joy makes us like God. Because it is for our profit. Because it is good for others.

II. The Joy Discriminated. "In the Lord."

A. As to sphere. "*In* the Lord." This is that sacred circle wherein a Christian's life should be always spent:

B. As to object. "In the *Lord*."

We should rejoice in the Lord God, Father, Son, and Spirit. We should rejoice in the Lord Jesus, dead, risen, etc. Not in temporals, personal, political, or pecuniary. Nor in self and its doings (Phil. 3:3).

III. The Time Appointed. "Always."

A. When you cannot rejoice in any other, rejoice in God.

B. When you can rejoice in other things, sanctify all with joy in God.

C. When you have not before rejoiced, begin at once.

D. When you have long rejoiced, do not cease for a moment.

E. When others are with you, lead them in this direction.

F. When you are alone, enjoy to the full this rejoicing.

IV. The Emphasis Laid on the Command. "Again I say, rejoice."

Paul rejoiced. He was habitually a happy man.

This epistle to the Philippians is peculiarly joyous. Let us look it through. The apostle is joyful throughout:

He sweetens prayer with joy (1:4).

He rejoices that Christ is preached (1:18).

He wishes to live to gladden the church (1:25).
To see the members like-minded with his joy (2:2).
It was his joy that he should not run in vain (2:16).
His farewell to them was, "Rejoice in the Lord" (3:1).
He speaks of those who rejoice in Christ Jesus (3:3).
He calls his converts his joy and his crown (4:1).
He expresses his joy in their kindness (4:4, 10, 18).

Upon working days rejoice in the Lord, who gives you strength to labor, and feeds you with the labor of your hands. On holidays rejoice in the Lord, who feeds you with the richness of His house. In plenty, rejoice again and again, because the Lord gives; in want rejoice, because the Lord takes away, and as it pleases the Lord, so come things to pass. —EDWARD MARBURY

The calendar of the sinner has only a few days in the year marked as festival days; but *every day* of the Christian's calendar is marked by the hand of God as a day of rejoicing. —ANON.

'Tis impious in a good man to be sad. —EDWARD YOUNG

Napoleon, when sent to Elba, adopted, in proud defiance of his fate, the motto, *Ubicunque felix*: It was not true in his case; but the Christian may be truly "happy everywhere" and always.

C. H. Spurgeon

Joy and Peace in Believing

Sometimes a light surprises
  The Christian while he sings;
It is the Lord who rises
  With healing in His wings:
When comforts are declining,
  He grants the soul again
A season of clear shining
  To cheer it after rain

In holy contemplation,
  We sweetly then pursue
The theme of God's salvation,
  And find it ever new:
Set free from present sorrow,
  We cheerfully can say,
E'en let th' unknown tomorrow
  Bring with it what it may.

It can bring with it nothing
  But He will bear us through;
Who gives the lilies clothing
  Will clothe His people too:
Beneath the spreading heavens,
  No creature but is fed;
And He who feeds the ravens
  Will give His children bread.

Though vine, nor fig tree neither,
  Their wonted fruit should bear,
Though all the fields should wither,
  Nor flocks, nor herds be there:
Yet God the same abiding,
  His praise shall tune my voice;
For while in Him confiding,
  I cannot but rejoice.

—*William Cowper*

IN EVERYTHING BY PRAYER

In nothing be anxious; but in everything by prayer (Phil. 4:6–7 ARV).

Worry robs the Christian of peace.

I. The Bane of Life Is Care.

You may be suffering, but your present affliction is never equal to your anxiety as to what may happen. Not events, but anxiety; not work, but worry is the bane of life. "I have had many troubles but most of them never happened." Suppose they do happen, they are never as bad as the anticipation.

II. The Cure of Care Is Prayer.

Prayer is the substitute for care. And you can make the substitute yourself. Prayer is not primarily an attempt to persuade God to change things, but rather an effort to bring us to quiet confidence.

You have seen, probably, the ferry across the stream where the boat has been pulled from shore to shore by its passengers laying hold on a cable stretched across. As they pull at the rope, of course, it does not move the banks toward the boat but the boat toward the banks. "Prayer in everything" is almost the equivalent of anxiety in nothing.

III. The End of Prayer Is Peace.

When Paul wrote the words of our text he was chained to a soldier, so it was easy for him to write about peace standing sentinel over our thoughts. The peace of God he had in mind is the peace which God has and gives. It cannot be described. "It passes understanding."

A student once went to see Phillips Brooks by appointment. He had a most important question for which he desired an answer. After the interview, as he was going home, he suddenly remembered that he had not asked the question. Nevertheless he was radiantly happy and he said, "Never mind. What I needed was not the solution of a special problem but the contagion of a triumphant spirit." *The end of prayer is peace.* It helps us to understand the meaning of our Master's promise: "My peace I give unto you."

Frederick Lent

CONSECRATION AND PRESERVATION

And the very God of peace sanctify you wholly; and I pray God your whole spirit and soul and body be preserved blameless unto the coming of our Lord Jesus Christ. Faithful is he that calleth you, who also will do it (1 Thess. 5:23–24).

Peace can be the portion of the child of God.

I. The Petition.

A. He prays for their sanctification—"Sanctify you wholly." The root idea of "sanctification," "holiness," "holy" and the like, is separation.

B. The extent of this consecration is noteworthy—"Sanctify you wholly."

C. He prays for their preservation—"Preserved blameless." The consecration is to be continually maintained in and for God.

D. The extent of this preservation—"Your whole spirit and soul and body." The spirit is that inmost part of our life which is related to God.

II. The Prerequisite.

A. "The God of peace Himself." The apostle stresses the fact that it is God "Himself" who consecrates and keeps us.

B. Further, God is described as "the God of peace." Only through peace can holiness come, and only as we have blessed personal experience of God as the God of peace can a prayer like this be answered.

III. The Prospect.

A. "Unto the coming of our Lord Jesus Christ." Once again the apostle prays with special reference to that glorious day to which he was always looking and pointing his readers.

B. There is no question in his mind.

IV. The Promise.

A. "Faithful is he that calleth you, who also will do it."

B. Lest we should think that so wonderful a prayer could not be fulfilled in daily experience, the apostle adds this blessed assurance that God, who puts this ideal before us, will enable us to realize it.

Selected

PATIENCE, COMFORT, AND HOPE
FROM THE SCRIPTURES

For whatsoever things were written aforetime were written for our learning, that we through patience and comfort of the Scriptures might have hope (Rom. 15:4).

The apostle declares that the Old Testament Scriptures are meant to teach New Testament believers.

Things written aforetime were written for our time.

The Old Testament is not out of date; apostles learned from it.

Nor has its authority ceased; it still teaches with certainty.

I. The Patience of the Scriptures.

A. Such as they inculcate:

Patience under every appointment of the divine will.

Patience under human persecution and satanic opposition.

Patience under brotherly burdens (Gal 6:2).

Patience in waiting for divine promises to be fulfilled.

B. Such as they exhibit in examples.

Job under many afflictions triumphantly patient.

Joseph patiently forgiving the unkindness of his brethren, and bearing the false accusation of his master.

David in many trials and under many reproaches, patiently waiting for the crown, and refusing to injure his persecutor.

Our Savior patient under all the many forms of trial.

II. The Comfort of the Scriptures.

A. Such as they inculcate:

They bid us to rise above fear (Ps. 46:1–3).

They urge us to think little of all transient things.

They command us to find our joy in God.

B. Such as they exhibit:

Enoch walking with God.

Abraham finding God his shield and exceeding great reward.

David strengthening himself in God.

Hezekiah spreading his letter before the Lord.

III. The Hope of the Scriptures.

Scripture is intended to work in us a good hope.

The hope of salvation (1 Thess. 5:8).

"The blessed hope, and the glorious appearing of our Lord" (Titus 2:13).

The hope of the resurrection of the dead (Acts 23:6).

The hope of glory (Col. 1:27).

How much important matter do we find condensed in this single verse! What a light and glory does it throw on the Word of God! It has been well noted, that we have here *its authority*, as it is a written word; *its antiquity*, as it was written aforetime; *its utility*, as it is written for our learning. —JAMES FORD

Oliver Cromwell once read aloud Philippians 4:11–13, and then remarked, "There, in the day when my poor child died, this Scripture did go nigh to save my life."

When George Peabody was staying at Sir Charles Reed's house, he saw the youngest child bringing to his father a large Bible for family prayers. Mr. Peabody said, "Ah! my boy, you carry your Bible now; but the time is coming when you will find that *the Bible must carry you.*"

"Speak to me now in Scripture language alone," said a dying Christian. "I can trust the words of God; but when they are words of man, it costs me an effort to think whether I may trust them."

—G. S. BOWES

As an instance of the patience, comfort, and hope, which come from the gospel, note the following from *Dr. Payson*: Christians might avoid much trouble if they would believe that God is able to make them happy without anything else. God has been depriving me one blessing after another; but as every one was removed, He has come in and filled up its place; and now, when I am a cripple, not able to move, I am happier than ever I was in my life before, or ever expected to be. If I had believed this twenty years ago, I might have been spared much anxiety.

C. H. Spurgeon

OUR GOD

Hebrews 12:29

1. The **"God of Patience"** to console us (Rom. 15:5).

2. The **"God of Peace"** to calm us (Rom. 15:33).

3. The **"God of Hope"** to cheer us (Rom. 15:13).

4. The **"God of all Comfort"** to comfort us (2 Cor. 1:3).

5. The **"God of Love"** to sustain us (2 Cor. 13:11).

6. The **"God of all Grace"** (1 Peter 5:10).

7. **"God and Father** of our Lord Jesus Christ" (Eph. 1:3).

F. E. Marsh

He Keeps the Key

Is there some problem in your life to solve,
  Some passage seeming full of mystery?
God knows, Who brings the hidden things to light,
  He keeps the key.

Is there some door closed by the Father's hand
  Which widely opened you had hoped to see?
Trust God and wait—for when He shuts the door,
  He keeps the key.

Is there some earnest prayer unanswered yet,
  Or answered *not* as you had thought 'twould be!
God will make clear His purpose by-and-by.
  He keeps the key.

Have patience with your God, your patient God,
  All wise, all knowing, no longer tarrier He,
And of the door of all thy future life
  He keeps the key.

Unfailing comfort, sweet and blessed rest,
  To know of *every* door He keeps the key.
That He at last when just *He* sees 'tis best,
    Will give it *thee.*

—Author Unknown

A MEDITATION ON KINDNESS

While I was musing the fire burned (Ps. 39:3).

It is better to have too much than too little feeling in our personal faith. We cannot love an unfeeling man. The feeling heart is the most human as well as the most humane part of humanity. But we admire it only when it leans upon a clear judgment and is thereby controlled.

There is much to be said in praise of quiet musing. We do not do much of it or see much of it in these days of rush and hurry. It has been said that meditation is a lost art. The order suggested here is musing, burning, speaking. "While I was musing the fire burned; then spake I with my tongue." Meditation encourages the most exalted feelings of devotion.

I. Some Proper Subjects of Meditation.
   A. The character of God.
   B. Providential dealings.
   C. The plan of salvation.
   D. Our relation to God.
   E. Our future.

II. Some Benefits of Meditation.
   A. The acquisition of spiritual power.
   B. The production of spiritual pleasure.
   C. The realization of religious hopes.

III. Meditation Is at Its Best When It Prepares Us for Action.
A. We are the better fitted to go back again to our active duties and demands.

B. We are made more *kind*, more *gentle*, more *forbearing*.

C. In musing we are taught a more correct knowledge of ourselves than we should otherwise possess, and may thus be fitted to have more power to correctly appraise and give aid to our neighbor.

Selected

PHARAOH'S KIND HOSPITALITY

*Regard not your stuff, for the good of all the land of Egypt is yours
(Gen. 45:20).*

We read that when Pharaoh learned that Joseph's father and brethren were suffering from famine in Palestine he kindly and generously invited them to make their home in Egypt. Lavish provision was made for their accommodation. Pharaoh furnished the wagons for their transportation and offered to supply them with everything they might need in the new country. He said, "Regard not your stuff, for the good of all the land of Egypt is yours."

1. That was certainly generous hospitality on the part of Pharaoh. We are not accustomed to think of anything so good as that from an Egyptian Pharaoh. Nevertheless hospitality is a most worthy grace.

2. This same occurrence also speaks well for Pharaoh's delicate consideration for Joseph. It was no doubt his high regard for Joseph that prompted the invitation. It shows the value he set upon Joseph.

3. It shows, too, how great is the influence of character. Joseph had proven himself not alone a man of great ability, but of unusual character and integrity.

4. Note also that when the brothers of Joseph returned to Palestine and extended Pharaoh's invitation to their father the father accepted. We read that "Israel took his journey with all that he had." He did not leave any of his "stuff" behind. He could not bear to leave it. He wanted all the old familiar furnishings wherever he might go. And there are a good many people today who cannot bear to leave behind any of the old "stuff" to which they have been accustomed. It is well for us to learn what old "stuff" in custom and habit and thought we had best leave behind.

Selected

GETTING RID OF THE CROOKED

To the pure you show yourself pure (Ps. 18:26 NIV).

This verse concludes, "To the crooked you show yourself crooked." The scholars agree that this is a valid translation.

1. One's idea of God is according to one's own bent. When my attitude and action are twisted as regards the brotherhood of man it is safe to say that I have a warped idea of the fatherhood of God. Can the unforgiving man plumb the deep wonder of the forgiveness of God? Can a man who hates his brother know the love of God? Can the hard man get any true idea of the tender mercy of God? Can the proud man understand the humility of Jesus?

2. This "twist" persists. Who has not noticed the persistence of a twist or the tendency to twist in a fabric or cord? So it is with our human natures. And that is perhaps one reason why our sanctification or growth in grace is so slow. It takes time to get rid of the twist.

3. But Christ is very patient. The good work He began with us will be completed. There is great joy in the new and larger vision of God which comes as one's perversity passes. "To the pure you show yourself pure." Blessed are the pure in heart [the untwisted]; for they shall see God."

M. K. W. Heicher

Do All the Good You Can

John Wesley had this for his rule of life:

> Do all the good you can,
> By all the means you can,
> In all the ways you can,
> In all the places you can,
> At all the times you can,
> To all the people you can,
> As long as ever you can.

THE LIFE WELL PLEASING TO GOD

How ye ought to walk and to please God (1 Thess. 4:1).

An answer. We ought to walk in:

1. **Personal purity** (vv. 3–8).

2. **Brotherly love** (vv. 9–10).

3. **Industry** (vv. 11–12).

4. **Quiet hope** concerning the unseen world and comfort for the bereaved (vv. 13–18).

Selected

GENTLENESS

Be gentle unto all men (2 Tim. 2:24).

I. Its Difficulty.
A. It is not generally appreciated.
B. It is not generally effective in bettering people.
C. We are provoked to the contrary.

II. Its Use. It has:
A. A developing power.
B. A consoling power.
C. A saving power.

III. Its Inducement.
A. We don't know who is in need of it.
B. We ourselves have received it of others.
C. We may be in need of it again.

Selected

FAITH: LIFE

Habakkuk 2:4; Romans 1:17;
Galatians 3:11; Hebrews 10:38

When the Spirit of God frequently repeats Himself, He thereby appeals for special attention. A doctrine so often declared must be of first importance. A doctrine so often asserted should be constantly preached. A doctrine so often proclaimed should be unhesitatingly received by each one of our hearers.

I. We Will Treat the Four Texts as One.

The teaching is clear. "The just shall live by his faith."

A. Life is received by the faith which makes a man just.

A man begins to live by a full acquittal from condemnation, and from penal death, so soon as he believes in Jesus. A man begins to live as one raised out of spiritual death so soon as he has faith in the Lord Jesus Christ.

B. Life is sustained by the faith which keeps a man just.

He who is forgiven and quickened lives ever afterward as he began to live—namely, by faith. He lives by faith in every condition:

1. In joy and in sorrow; in wealth and in poverty;
2. In strength and in weakness; in laboring and in languishing; in life and in death.
3. He lives best when faith is at its best, even though in other respects he may be sorely put to it. He lives the life of Christ most blessedly when most intensely he believes in Christ.

II. We Will Treat the Four Texts Separately.

If we read with precision, we shall see that Scripture contains no repetitions. The context gives freshness of meaning to each apparent repetition.

A. Our first text (Hab. 2:4) exhibits faith as enabling a man to live on in peace and humility, while as yet the promise has not come to its maturity. While waiting we live by faith, and not by sight.

We are thus able to bear up under the temporary triumphs of the wicked.

We are thus preserved from proud impatience at delay.

2. Our second text (Rom. 1:17) exhibits faith as working salvation from the evil which is in the world through lust. The chapter in which it stands presents an awful view of human nature, and implies that only faith in the gospel can bring us life in the form of—

Mental enlightenment of life as to the true God (Rom. 1:19–23).

Moral purity of life (Rom. 1:24ff.).

C. Our third text (Gal. 3:11) exhibits faith as bringing to us that justification which saves us from the sentence of death. Nothing can be plainer, more positive, more sweeping than this declaration that no man is justified before God except by faith. Both the negative and the positive are plain enough.

D. Our fourth text (Heb. 10:38) exhibits faith as the life of final perseverance.

There is need of faith while waiting for heaven (vv. 32–36).

The absence of such faith would cause us to draw back (v. 38).

That drawing back would be a fatal sign.

That drawing back can never occur, for faith saves the soul from all hazards, keeping its face heavenwards even to the end.

What can you do who have no faith?

In what other way can you be accepted with God?

On what ground can you excuse your unbelief in your God?

Will you perish sooner than believe Him?

The Jews in the Talmud have the saying, "The whole law was given to Moses at Sinai, in six hundred and thirteen precepts." David, in the fifteenth Psalm, brings them all within the compass of eleven. Isaiah brings them to six (Isa. 33:15); Micah to three (Mic. 6:8); Isaiah, again, to two (Isa. 56); Habakkuk to this one, "The just shall live by his faith." —LIGHTFOOT

The soul is the life of the body. Faith is the life of the soul. Christ is the life of faith. —FLAVEL

> Inscribed upon the portal from afar
> Conspicuous as the brightness of a star,
> Legible only by the light they give
> Stand the soul-quickening words—
> *Believe and Live.*

To believe God is not a little thing; it is the index of a heart reconciled to God, and the token of true spirituality of mind; it is the essence of true worship, and the root of sincere obedience. He who believes his God in spite of his sins, does him more honor than cherubim and seraphim in their continual adoration.

A little thing faith! How is it then that unbelief is so great a crime that it is marked out for reprobation as the one damning evil which shuts men out of heaven? Whatever else you put in the second place, give faith the lead; it is not a vain thing, for it is your life.

C. H. Spurgeon

FAITHFULNESS IN SERVICE

Do all to the glory of God (1 Cor. 10:31).

Corinth was a city of idols. Christ's new followers were to do all to the glory of God. Here Paul is calling them to faithfulness in service.

I. The Depth of This Principle:

God is Lord of all, and we ought to use all things for His glory. Christ said, "I have glorified thee." Only life can become the true medium. Do all things in a nobler spirit, in fellowship with him, and with one desire—to please Him. The true end of life is God Himself.

II. Its Penetration:

Give me something important to do—and the text speaks of duties that are of microscopic fineness. Something religious—and God sends us down to the plains to live and work for Him. Something quick and spectacular—and we remember Jesus, who on God's business went back home to be a carpenter, a devoted son, and a loyal brother. Go on being happy, but remember that life must first serve God.

III. Its Comprehensiveness:

Everything we do is the expression of self, and so may every action be an offering unto God. What nobility this lends to life! There is nothing trivial about it. Every little detail has its place in the great consummation. He wants not success but faithfulness!

Selected

UNITY IN CHRIST

Examine yourselves, whether ye be in the faith; prove your own selves.
Know ye not your own selves, how that Jesus Christ is in you, except ye
be reprobates (2 Cor. 13:5).

The state of faith is here described as having Christ dwelling in us.

I. The Very First Act of Faith Is Represented in the Scriptures as Receiving, Appropriating Christ.

The believer accepts Christ primarily as his Redeemer. But he accepts at the same time the entire teaching of Christ and embodies that in his manner of living. That, in a sentence, is what it means to bear fruit as a Christian.

II. The Believer's Actions Are Manifestations of the Indwelling Christ.

The motives for these actions arise from the Christ-spirit within. They are, like Christ's own acts, entirely unselfish. Accordingly, when Christians are found doing something which does not agree with their profession, or when they fail to appreciate what other Christians are doing, it is pertinent to inquire whether they are still in a state of faith and grace.

III. Every Christian Readily Understands Any Other Christian.

Just as readily he should agree and cooperate with him. For Christ, though dwelling in many persons who may differ in external matters, is never a divided Christ. The Christ in the heart of the primitive native is the same Christ as He in the heart of the missionary who ministers to him.

IV. There Are Differences Among Christians Which Do Not Necessarily Disturb the Peace and Healthy Development of the Church.

But when the differences touch the Christian vitality, the Christ in us, it is necessary that a thorough self-examination be made.

Selected

A FOCUS ON FAITH

But before faith came, we were kept under the law, shut up unto the faith which should afterwards be revealed (Gal. 3:23).

Here we have a condensed history of the world before the gospel of the grace of God was fully revealed by the coming of our Lord Jesus. This history of each saved soul is a miniature likeness of the story of the ages. God acts upon the same principles both with the race and with individuals.

I. The Unhappy Period: "Before faith came."

A. We had no idea of faith by nature. It would never occur to the human mind that we could be saved by believing in Jesus.

B. When we heard of faith as the way of salvation we did not understand it. We could not persuade ourselves that the words used by the preacher had their common and usual meaning.

C. We saw faith in others, and wondered at its results; but we could not exercise it for ourselves.

D. The reason for this inability was moral, not mental: We were proud, and did not care to renounce self-righteousness. We could not grasp the notion of salvation by faith, because it was contrary to the usual run of our opinions.

II. The Custody We Were In: "Kept under the law, shut up."

A. We were always within the sphere of law. In fact, there is no getting out of it. As all the world was only one prison for a man who offended Caesar, so is the whole universe no better than a prison for a sinner.

B. We were always kicking against the bounds of the law, sinning, and pining because we could not sin more.

C. We dared not overleap it altogether and defy its power. Thus, in the case of many of us, it checked us and held us captive with its irksome forbiddings and commandings.

D. We could not find rest. The law awakened conscience; fear and shame attend such an awakening.

E. We could not even fall into the stupor of despair; for the law excited life, though it forbade hope.

III. The Revelation Which Set Us Free: "The faith which should afterwards be revealed."

The only thing which could bring us out of prison was faith. Faith came, and then we understood—
A. What was to be believed.
  Salvation by Another.
  Salvation of a most blessed sort, gloriously sure, and complete.
  Salvation by a most Glorious Person.
B. What it was to believe.
  We saw that it was "trust," implicit and sincere.
  We saw that it was ceasing from self and obeying Christ.
C. Why we believed.
  We were shut up to this one way of salvation.
  We were shut out of every other.
  We were compelled to accept free grace or perish.

The law and the gospel are two keys. The law is the key that shuts up all men under condemnation, and the gospel is the key which opens the door and lets them out. —WILLIAM TYNDALE

The law is made to act the part of a sentry, guarding every avenue but one, and that one leads those who are compelled to take it to the faith of the gospel. They are shut up to this faith as their only alternative—like an enemy driven by the superior tactics of an opposing general, to take up the only position in which they can maintain themselves, or fly to the only town in which they can find a refuge or a security. This seems to have been a favorite style of argument with Paul, and the way in which he often carried on an intellectual warfare with the enemies of his Master's cause. It forms the basis of that masterly and decisive train of reasoning which we have in his epistle to the Romans.

The law was meant to prepare men for Christ, by showing them that there is no other way of salvation except through Him. It had two special ends: the first was to bring the people who lived under it into a consciousness of the deadly dominion of sin, to shut them up, as it were, into a prison house out of which only one door of escape should be visible, namely, the door of faith in Jesus.

The second intention was to fence about and guard the chosen race to whom the law was given—to keep as a peculiar people separate from all the world, so that at the proper time the gospel of Christ might spring forth, and go out from them as the joy and comfort of the whole human race.　　　　　　—T. G. ROOKE

C. H. Spurgeon

THE BELIEVER'S GROWTH IN FAITH

With the heart man believeth unto righteousness (Rom. 10:10).

We partially know about God by thinking; we fully know Him only by believing. Theories will change, but heart experiences of the divine presence in the soul are the same as when God walked with Adam in Eden. The feelings of sin and sorrow, of joy and peace, are common to all ages, and all hearts.

I.　There can be no evolution in the nature of love and faith. The only change may be in the evermore increasing volume. The Lord's Prayer is hallowed for the heart. God's love shed abroad in the heart makes all Christians one in him.

An American who met a heathen convert in India saw the light of peace and joy on his face. They recognized each other as followers of Jesus, but they could not convey by words the likeness of their experience, except that there are two words which are the same in all languages; so one said "Amen" and the other, "Hallelujah!" Thus a single word may express volumes of heart experience, because it awakens similar feelings in consciousness.

II.　While the mind is often lost in the labyrinths of speculation, the heart, through the telescope of faith, sees the Father's home a palace of splendor at the end of the way, and feels the joy unspeakable and full of glory.

III.　The way of the doubter is hard and gloomy, but the way of faith is the path of hope and leads to everlasting triumph.

Selected

PRIDE
(THE OPPOSITE OF HUMILITY)

Be not proud (Jer. 13:15).

Let us look at the nature of humility by examining its opposite—pride.

1. There is race pride.

2. There is face pride.

3. There is place pride.

4. There is grace pride.

5. Pride is abhorrent to God.

6. Pride is unlike Christ.

7. Pride ruins. Pride goes before a fall.

Selected

PRIDE THE DESTROYER;
HUMILITY REWARDED

Behold, his soul which is lifted up is not upright in him: but the just shall live by his faith (Hab. 2:4).

Delay of deliverance is a weighing of men.

Suspense is very trying, and constitutes a searching test.

This divides men into two classes by bringing out their real character.

The contrast between the proud and the just is striking; the arrogant and the upright are poles apart; and the result of trial in the two cases is as different as death from life.

The tarrying of the promise—

I. Reveals a Great Fault. "His soul which is lifted up."

The man is impatient, and will not endure to wait. This is pride full-blown, for it quarrels with the Lord, and dares to dictate to Him.

A. It is very natural to us to be proud. So our first ancestors fell, and we inherit their fault.

B. Pride takes many shapes, and among the rest this vainglorious habit of thinking that we ought to be waited on at once.

C. In all cases pride is unreasonable. Who are we that God should make Himself our servant, and read His time from our watch?

II. Discovers a Serious Opposition.

He grows tired of the gospel, which is the sum of the promises, and he becomes averse to the exercise of the faith which it requires. His pride makes him reject salvation by grace, through faith in Jesus.

A. He is too great to consider it.

B. He is too wise to believe it.

C. He is too good to need it.

D. He is too advanced in "culture" to endure it.

III. Directs Us to a Pleasing Contrast.

A. The man who is really just is truly humble.

B. Being humble, he does not dare to doubt his God, but yields to His Word an implicit faith.

C. His faith keeps him alive under trial, and conducts him in the joys and privileges of spiritual life.

D. His life conquers the trial, and develops into life eternal.

As the first step heavenward is *humility*, so the first step hellward is *pride*. Pride counts the gospel foolishness, but the gospel always shows pride to be so. Shall the sinner be proud who is going to hell? Shall the saint be proud who is newly saved from it? God had rather His people fared poorly than lived proudly.   —MASON

Poverty of spirit is the bag into which Christ puts the riches of His grace.   —ROWLAND HILL

We must be emptied of self before we can be filled with grace; we must be stripped of our rags before we can be clothed with righteousness; we must be unclothed that we may be clothed; wounded, that we may be healed; killed, that we may be made alive; buried in disgrace, that we may rise in holy glory. These words, "Sown in corruption, that we may be raised in incorruption; sown in dishonor, that we may be raised in glory; sown in weakness, that we may be raised in power," are as true of the soul as of the body.

To borrow an illustration from the surgeon's art: the bone that is set wrong must be broken again, in order that it may be set aright. I press this truth on your attention. It is certain that a soul filled with self has no room for God; and like the inn at Bethlehem, crowded with meaner guests, a heart preoccupied by pride and her godless train, has no chamber within which Christ may be born in us "the hope of glory." —GUTHRIE

But for pride, the angels who are in hell should be in heaven (Jude 6); but for pride, Nebuchadnezzar, who is in the forest, should be in his palace (Dan. 4); but for pride, Pharaoh, who lies with the fishes, should be with his nobles (Ex. 14); no sin has pulled so many down as this, which promised to set them up.

But for pride, the Pharisees would have received Christ as gently as His disciples; but for pride, Herod would have worshiped Christ as humbly as the shepherds. Thus pride can be seen as the opposite of humility (meekness), and is in direct contrast to that rare characteristic.

C. H. Spurgeon

GROWING IN HIS LIKENESS

Learn of me, for I am meek and lowly in heart: and ye shall find rest unto your souls (Matt. 11:29).

It is not in us, but in Christ, that we find the source of deep, pure, humble, spiritual rest.

I. The Diligent, Teachable Soul Drinks in His Brimming Cup of Wisdom and Knowledge.

His highest ideals can be absorbed as the earth absorbs the sun and shower. Of ourselves we can do nothing, however. "It is not I but Christ that liveth in me." We become conscious of the importance of fellowship and partnership with Him.

II. We Know That God Is in Christ and Christ in Us.

We are evermore abiding in unity, bound by cords of love. It is then we have the power to practice the presence of the Master, showing forth His light to men. Let us therefore humble ourselves in Christlike meekness, that we may be exalted. He made Himself of no reputation that He might lift a race to exaltation.

III. **Then No Man Should Speak of Having Made Sacrifices in Becoming a Christian.**

IV. **Then an Heir of God Should Be Made "meet for his inheritance."**

Without a "meetness" for it, the inheritance would be a burden rather than a blessing. Our business here is to cultivate the manners, to learn the language, and acquire the attitudes of our future abode.

V. **Then, in Securing This Meetness, the Christian May Confidently Expect Divine Aid.**

As soon doubt the rising of the sun as to think that God would fail to aid and bless the man who is struggling to be pure and Christlike.

Selected

A WATCHWORD

Arise, let us go hence (John 14:31).

Our Lord was under marching orders, and He knew it: for Him there was no permanent place upon this earth.

Hear how He calls Himself, and all His own, to move on, though bloody sweat and bloody death be in the way. He calls us to humility.

I. **Our Master's Watchword.**

By this stirring word—

A. He expressed His desire to obey the Father.

He was not hindered by expected suffering.

B. He indicated His readiness to meet the archenemy, "The Prince of this world cometh. Arise, let us go hence."

He was prepared for the test. He "hath nothing in Me."

He revealed His practical activity. All through the chapter observe our Lord's energy. He is ever on the move. "I go. I will come again. I will do it. I will pray. Arise, let us go hence."

He prefers action to the most sacred rites, and so leaves the supper table with this word on His lips.

He prefers action to the sweetest converse. "I will not talk much with you. Arise, let us go hence."

II. Our Own Motto. "Arise, let us go hence."

Ever onward, ever forward, we must go (Ex. 14:15).

A. Out of the world when first called by grace (2 Cor. 6:17).

B. Out of forbidden associations, if, as believers, we find ourselves like Lot in Sodom. "Escape for thy life" (Gen. 19:17).

C. Out of present attainments when growing in grace (Phil. 3:13–14).

D. Out of all rejoicing in self. There we must never stop for a single instant. Self-satisfaction should not tempt us.

E. To suffer when the Lord lays affliction upon us (2 Cor. 12:9).

F. To die when the voice from above calls us home (2 Tim. 4:6).

It was well said once by a remarkable man, and the words are worth remembering, "Bear in mind that you are just then beginning to go wrong when you are a little pleased with yourself because you are going right." Let us watch against this as a snare of Satan, and endeavor ever to maintain the apostolic attitude: "In lowliness of mind, let each esteem other better than himself."

And let me caution you not to make the mistake of supposing that this self-complacency can be effectually guarded against by a mere use of the recognized theological expressions duly ascribing all the merit and all the praise to God . . . [which may be] spiritual pride . . . not true humility.

C. H. Spurgeon

THE MEANING OF HUMILITY

Be not highminded, but fear (Rom. 11:20).

In today's language we would say, Don't be high-hat or get on your high-horse. There are other ways of expressing it. Don't be proud or haughty. Don't be pompous or arrogant. Don't swagger or strut. One thing is sure, that *humility* and dependence on God are essential to the Christian character. The opposite, pride and self-sufficiency, are to be avoided. They will lead to humiliation and shame. "Be not highminded, but fear."

I. Let Us Think, First, of the Evil to Be Avoided.

"Be not highminded." There are different sorts of highmindedness. There are highminded persons who boast of the dignity and wealth of their ancestors, of the excellency of their birth, and therefore think themselves superior to others who have no lofty or distinguished lineage to boast of.

Those are highminded who have too great opinions of themselves and are fond of human applause. Haughtiness of mind characterized the Pharisees of old. They dearly loved human applause. When they gave alms they sounded a trumpet before them. They trusted in themselves that they were righteous and despised others.

Even Christians are in danger from this sin. There is such a thing as pride of wealth, or of superior circumstances in life. There is such a thing as pride of talent.

If a man has superior knowledge, discernment, or use of eloquent speech, he is in danger of being puffed up.

There is even such a thing as pride of usefulness. Many a very useful man is in danger of attributing too much to himself, instead of ascribing the whole of his success to God, who alone can give the increase. Where is boasting, then? It is excluded. Boast not of what you are, of what you do, of what you give.

II. Notice, Second, That We Are Given a Means for Avoiding This Evil.

"Be not highminded, but fear." This fear implies prudence, vigilance, watchfulness. Such fear is represented as a holy affection, a gracious habit produced by divine power in the heart. Avoid the awful effects of pride, for it is the forerunner of destruction. As creatures, our insignificance should make us humble; but as sinners we have reason to be still more so.

Selected

NUMBERING OUR DAYS

So teach us to number our days, that we may apply our hearts unto wisdom (Ps. 90:12).

I. The Duty Suggested: "Number our days."
A. Number their fewness.
B. Number their fleetness.
C. Number their uncertainty.

II. The Prayer Inspired: "So teach us to number."
A. Suggested by the flight of the seasons.
B. By the prevalence of mortality around us.
C. By the lessons of the Scriptures.
D. By the influence of the Holy Spirit.

III. The End to Be Attained: "That we may apply our hearts unto wisdom."
A. That we may apply our hearts vigorously. That is what "apply" means.

B. That we may apply our hearts immediately. Yes, no delay. The immediate, and very desirable, duty of performance.

Selected

WHOLENESS AS AN ATTAINMENT

I hate men who are half and half (Ps. 119:113 MOFFATT'S TRANSLATION).

I. Let Us Desire Wholeness.
In living with our loved ones and friends the wholeness which is wholesomeness is desirable. We think on truth, honor, justice, purity, loveliness, kindness. Let them do their perfect work in us that our lives may spread virtue to others.

II. In Relation to One's Self, Wholeness Is Health.
The two words are related in the Old Anglo-Saxon. When Jesus cured a certain man it is written that he made him whole. It is an open secret that health often lies, not in half-and-halfness, but in out-and-outness, integration.

III. Wholeness Before God in Holiness.

Those who shy at so pious a word may be led to revise their opinion when they consider that holiness or wholeness means integration—a personality integrated by God's forces. Who would not seek such holiness?

M. K. W. Heicher

MAGNIFICENT CONTROL

Choose you a man (1 Sam. 17:8).

To fell the giant, David used only one stone. That was magnificent control. With five stones in his bag, he used one!

I. It Isn't Just by Chance That a Man Shows Magnificent Control.

When they said, "Thou art not able to go against this Philistine to fight," David replied, "Once when a lion attacked my father's flock I slew him." Control is an attainment.

II. A Man Who Has Temper Should Have Control.

Thank God for temper. It means that one is not sluggish, not placid, not easygoing, not sparkless, not spineless. Temper-controlling men are very useful in the purposes of Christ.

III. Our Desires Need Such Control.

They are often instinctive, not evil; they carry energy which can be put to high and noble use. Through this energy, harnessed, manhood becomes princely and powerful, and womanhood gathers charm and royalty.

IV. We Should Control Our Fears.

Fear sublimated into courage can fell a Goliath with one stone.

The developing of magnificent control is one of the glorious capacities of the gospel.

M. K. W. Heicher

MOUNTING UP WITH WINGS

They shall mount up with wings as eagles (Isa. 40:31).

I. Wings Are Supremely Necessary.

That is, if you want to rise above the dead level.

II. Wings Are Marvelously Delicate.

The first wings that ever attracted my attention were locust wings, thinner than paper and transparent. The ribs, like those of a tender leaf, were so fragile that a baby's hand could have broken them. Thinner than paper, yet 200 strokes a second!

III. Wings Are Exquisitely Controlled.

The crow flaps its wings in clear weather; when the weather changes it glides. The wild duck takes twice as long for the spreading downbeat of its wings as it does for the upbeat.

IV. Wings Are Gloriously Free.

They are free to adventure. With wings the eagle may poise on the topmost crag of the High Sierras. With wings a lone eagle flew across the Atlantic waters.

When the ancient prophet wrote, "They shall mount up with wings as eagles," he referred particularly to youth. Prophecy always waits for someone to say, "That means me—I'll put truth into prophecy."

1. If wings are supremely necessary, then I'll use them—the wing of character and the wing of vocation. There are some ants that are born with wings but they cannot use them for the glory and rapture of flight; they tear them off and go through their whole lives as crawling insects.

2. If wings are marvelously useful, I'll plume them. Birds preen their wings to keep themselves clean and in good condition. Jesus, the world's Savior, kept His wing of character spotless, also His vocation wing, His Saviorhood.

3. If wings are exquisitely controlled, I'll fasten them in a keel. The perfect control of the wing comes from its connection to that strong bone of the bird's breast shaped like a keel. It is when one's character and vocation are anchored in Christ that he has exquisite control.

4. If my wings are gloriously free I'll be able to live gloriously.

M. K. W. Heicher

THE UNTAMED SOUL

A wild ass alone by himself (Hos. 8:9).

What a figure of the untamed soul who refuses the easy yoke of God! Man's untamed spirit spurns the God of love. You cannot conceive a truer picture of the one who is altogether intractable than this of the "wild ass alone by himself." The wild ass will go his own way. So the untamed soul.

Ephraim and the ten tribes are compared to the wild ass for many reasons.

I. They Refused God's Services.

Their hearts were untamed; they were stubborn in their rejection of Gods inviting grace. They were full of obdurate folly. They were headstrong and unruly, not consenting to any restraints. The wild ass traverses the desert only to gratify its own low nature. Picture of the untamed, intractable soul.

II. The Wild Ass Is Excessively Swift.

Although numbers commonly herd together, yet it is not unusual for some one of them to break away and separate himself from his company and run alone or at random. It is when he thus breaks away by himself, seeking thereby to be masterless and free, that he is in a fair way of being left to his own devices.

III. As the Wild Ass Is the Lion's Prey in the Wilderness, so

the untamed soul, faithless to God, seeking its own things, or things for himself alone, for his own gratification, his own pleasure, is most liable to come to destruction. Only those who submit themselves to God's control achieve self-control.

Selected

HAVING GOALS

Save yourselves from this untoward generation (Acts 2:40).

The word "untoward" is the opposite of toward. When one goes *toward* a place one is moving in the direction of that place.

I. Untoward Movement Is Movement That Is Not Getting Anywhere!

It may movement in a circle merry-go-round movement. It may be the natural movement of a man that is lost.

II. A Whole Generation May Be Going in Circles.

One must save one's self from it to get ahead of it. The drag of the crowd is terrific. The circle of conformity is deadly. Jesus might have slipped into the Pharisee's circle. Paul did for a time move in that circle, but he broke from it.

III. The First Step in Breaking from a Go-nowhere Generation Is to Catch Sight of a Goal.

Such a goal Jesus can give us. Jesus can give an objective, an objective embedded in the heart of reality. Let's go. Let's not merely go places. Let's go some place. There is such a goal and one can come at it. That is what religion can do for us. We know where we are going and we are on the way.

M. K. W. Heicher

"I OF CHRIST"

I of Christ (1 Cor. 1:12).

In this message we will not speak of sects and parties and divisions, but of consecration to Christ. Parties may be right when they stand on the common foundations of Christ; when they esteem, love, and help each other; when they exhibit a holy emulation in exalting Christ. They are wrong when they exalt party names and differences above Christ; when they are slavishly attached to their party and make it the great object of their zeal; when they note and despise others and exclude them from their fellowship; when they seek to glorify their party above all others.

But let us see what "I of Christ" means as a personal declaration.

It means:

1. I own His divine mission.
2. I acknowledge His essential dignity.
3. I believe in His doctrines.
4. I rely on His sacrifice.
5. I love His Person.
6. I obey His will.

Selected

THE HEAVENLY RACE

So run, that ye may obtain (1 Cor. 9:24).

I. The Requisites Necessary to Our Running the Heavenly Race.

A. A clear view of divine things. To know the way of truth in opposition to error. To know the way of holiness in opposition to wickedness.

B. A well-studied and regular preparation. Strict discipline; cast off every encumbrance.

C. Vigorous and persevering diligence.

II. The Happiness of Those Who Persevere to the End.

A. A crown of victory. Christ will bestow it.

B. A kingdom of glory. The place, inhabitants, and Sovereign of that kingdom are glorious.

Selected

Know Yourself

The ancient Greeks knew that "the unexamined life is not worth living." Over the Greek Temple at Delphi the words were inscribed: "Know thyself." They knew the importance of self-knowledge as the key to all other knowledge.

BOUGHT WITH A PRICE

And ye are not your own, for ye are bought with a price: therefore glorify God in your body, and in your spirit, which are God's (1 Cor. 6:19–20).

With what ardor does the apostle pursue sin to destroy it! He is not so prudish as to let sin alone, but cries out, in plain language, "Flee fornication." The shame is not in the rebuke, but in the sin which calls for it.

He chases this awful wickedness with arguments (see v. 18).

He drags it into the light of the Spirit of God. "What? Know ye not that your body is the temple of the Holy Ghost?" (v. 19).

He says it at the cross. "Ye are bought with a price."

Let us consider this last argument, that we may find therein death for our sins.

I. A Blessed Fact: "Ye are bought with a price."

"Ye are bought." This is that idea of redemption which modern heretics dare to style *mercantile*. The mercantile redemption is the scriptural one; for the expression, "bought with a price," is a double declaration of that idea.

A. This is either a fact or not. "Ye are bought, or ye are unredeemed." Terrible alternative.

B. If a fact, it is *the* fact of your life. A wonder of wonders.

C. It will remain to you eternally the greatest of all facts. If true at all, it will never cease to be true, and it will never be outdone in importance by any other event.

D. It should therefore operate powerfully upon us both now and ever.

II. A Plain Consequence: "Ye are not your own."

Negative. It is clear that if bought, ye are *not* your own.

A. This involves privilege.

You are not your own provider: sheep are fed by their shepherd.

You are not your own guide: ships are steered by their pilot.

B. This also involves responsibility.

We are not our own to injure. Neither body nor soul.

Not our own to waste, in idleness, amusement, or speculation.

Not our own to exercise caprice, and follow our own prejudices, depraved affections, wayward wills, or irregular appetites.

Positive. "Your body and your spirit, which are God's." We are altogether God's. Body and spirit include the whole man.

We are always God's. The price once paid, we are forever His.

III. A Practical Conclusion: "Glorify God in your body, and in spirit, which are God's."

Glorify God *in your body.*

By cleanliness, chastity, temperance, industry, cheerfulness, self-denial, patience, etc.

Glorify God—

In a suffering body by patience unto death.

In a working body by holy diligence.

In a worshiping body by bowing in prayer.

In a well-governed body by self-denial.

In an obedient body by doing the Lord's will with delight.

Glorify God *in your spirit.*

By holiness, faith, zeal, love, heavenliness, cheerfulness, fervor, humility, expectancy, etc.

But why should so vast a price be required? Is man worth the cost? A man may be bought in parts of the world for the value of an ox. It was not man simply, but man in a certain relation, that had to be redeemed. See one who has been all his days a drunken, idle, worthless fellow. All appropriate to him the epithet "worthless"—worth nothing.

But that man commits a crime for which he is sentenced to be hanged or to be imprisoned for life. Go and try to buy him now. Redeem him and make him your servant. Let the richest man in town offer all the money he possesses for that worthless man, and his offer would be wholly vain, why? Because now there is not only the man to be considered, but the law. It needs a very great price to redeem one man from the curse of the law; but Christ came to redeem all men from the curse of the Divine law. —WILLIAM ROBINSON

C. H. Spurgeon

THE SPIRIT WE NEED IN A WARRING WORLD

God hath not given us the spirit of fear; but of power, and of love, and of a sound mind (2 Tim. 1:7).

The words of Paul the aged to his young friend Timothy. The Christian will not deliberately court danger, but if danger comes upon him he must remain calm, steadfast, and unafraid, allowing the fruits of the Spirit to fill his life.

1. The Spirit of God Is Not a Spirit of Fear, but of Power.

"We wrestle not against flesh and blood," etc. God is greater than the massed forces of evil.

2. The Spirit of God Is a Spirit of Love.

If you want to know what the spirit of love is read 1 Corinthians 13.

3. The Spirit of God Is a Spirit of Sanity.

The R.V. here has "discipline." Yes, now is the time for discipline. Refusing to get excited or panic-stricken, even in face of danger. Doing things calmly and unhurriedly, yet quickly and efficiently. The spirit of God is a spirit of sanity in an insane world, which has been cynically described as "the greatest outdoor lunatic asylum in the universe." But the spirit of God will keep us sane and sound in our thinking, even amidst the madness of war.

May we receive God's spirit of power and love—and sanity!—and know that underneath are the everlasting arms!

Selected

Drought

My heart is parched by unbelief,
  My spirit dry from inward strife;
The heavens above are turned to brass,
  Arid and fruitless is my life.

Then falls Thy rain, O Holy One;
  Fresh is the earth, and young once more;
Then falls Thy Spirit on my heart;
  My life is green; the drought is o'er!
  —Betty Bruechert

ETERNAL RICHES

So is he who lays up treasure for himself, and is not rich toward God
(Luke 12:21).

What is the implication of this verse? It is possible to be rich toward God. Some other questions arise from this verse.

I. Who Is He That Is Rich Toward God?
Some answers:
A. He who is rich in the estimation of God.
B. He who is rich in the favor of God.
C. He who is rich in the graces that God imparts.
D. He who is rich in a title to the inheritance which God has promised.

II. Who Is He Who Lays Up Treasures for Himself?
A. He whose ruling passion is the accumulating of worldly wealth.
B. He who expends or employs his wealth only for his selfish gratification.

III. Wherein lies the foolishness of him who is not rich toward God, but lays up treasure for himself?
A. In that his wealth does not make him happy while he retains it.
B. In that his wealth may be snatched from him by innumerable casualties.
C. In that his wealth must be resigned at death, and all must die. To the worldling, how unhappy.

How urgent the need of better blessings than the world can give. To believers, how thankful they should be for the better and more enduring substance of the fruits of the Spirit revealed in the life of the devout Christian. To all, how desirable it is that we should be eager to be rich toward God.

Selected

"LETS" WHICH LET IN A BLESSING

1. **Vigilance**. "Let your loins be girded about" (Luke 12:35).

2. **Diligence**. "Let every man prove his own work" (Gal. 6:4).

3. **Continuance**. "Let us not be weary in well-doing" (Gal. 6:9).

4. **Dominance**. "Let the peace of God rule in your hearts" (Col. 3:15).

5. **Sustenance**. "Let the Word of Christ dwell in you richly" (Col. 3:16).

6. **Endurance**. "Let us run with patience the race" (Heb. 12:1).

7. **Supplication**. "Let your requests be made known unto God" (Phil. 4:6).

8. **Utterance**. "Let your speech be always with grace" (Col. 4:6).

F. E. Marsh

Go On!

But that which ye have already hold fast till I come.
—Rev. 2:25

> One step won't take you very far;
> You've got to keep on walking;
> One word won't tell folks who you are;
> You've got to keep on talking;
> One inch won't make you very tall;
> You've got to keep on growing;
> One deed won't do it all;
> You've got to keep on going.
> —*Arkansas Baptist*

LETTING THE LIGHT SHINE AT HOME

"Go home" (Mark 5:19) "and show how great things God hath done unto thee" (Luke 8:39). It is in the home we need to have—

1. **Our speech** seasoned with the salt of grace, that we may speak sweetly (Col. 4:6).

2. **Our manners** tempered with the grace of courteousness, that we may act graciously (1 Peter 3:8).

3. **Our behavior** toned with the godliness of chastity that we may attract powerfully (1 Peter 3:1–2).

4. **Our conduct** tuned with the Word of God, that we may act consistently (Titus 2:1–14).

5. **Our rule** ruled with the authority of heaven, that we may behave consecratingly (1 Tim. 3:1–7).

6. **Our office** dominated with the beauty of faithfulness, that we may live blamelessly (1 Tim. 3:8–13).

7. **Our relations** in life adjusted with the direction of the Spirit, that we may show we have received the Spirit fully (Col. 3:17; 4:1; Eph. 5:18; 6:9).

F. E. Marsh

Dedication

BEETHOVEN is unsurpassed in his painstaking fidelity to his music. Hardly a bar of his was not written and rewritten at least a dozen times. JOSEF HAYDN, through much hardship, produced over 800 musical compositions, and at age 66 gave the world that matchless oratorio "The Creation."

SCHUMANN-HEINK's parents were so poor they could not afford a good piano but a dilapidated old one. For 20 years she fought off poverty to become one of the world's greatest singers.

MICHELANGELO's "Last Judgment," one of the twelve master paintings of the ages, was the product of 8 years' unremitting toil. Over 2,000 studies of it were found among his papers. And LEONARDO DA VINCI worked on "The Last Supper" for 10 years, often so absorbed he forgot to eat for whole days.

—Selected

No devoted Christian can do anything unworthy of the name he bears. He *must* live out and show the fruits of the Spirit:

1. As a **Child** of God, he is obedient to his Father (1 Peter 1:14–17).

2. As a **Citizen** of heaven, he is separated from the evils of earth (1 Peter 2:11; Heb. 11:13).

3. As a **Called One**, he is walking worthy of his high and holy calling (1 Thess. 2:12).

4. As a **Charged Servant**, he is faithful to the trust committed to him (1 Tim. 1:18; 5:21; 6:13; 2 Tim. 4:1).

5. As a **Chosen Vessel**, he is selected to be for God's use and service (Acts 9:15; 2 Tim. 2:4; 1 Peter 2:9).

6. As a **Consecrated Believer**, he is wholly devoted to the Lord Himself (Num. 6:7–9, 12; 2 Chron. 29:31).

7. As a **Covenanted Priest**, he is fearless in his fidelity to his Lord (Mal. 2:4–5; Heb. 8:10).

F. E. Marsh

Devotion

NOAH WEBSTER labored 36 years writing his *Dictionary*, crossing the Atlantic twice to gather material.

MILTON rose at 4:00 A.M. every day in order to have enough hours for his *Paradise Lost*. GIBBON spent 26 years on his *Decline and Fall of the Roman Empire*. BRYANT rewrote one of his poetic masterpieces 99 times before publication and it became a classic.

ADAM CLARK spent 40 years writing his *Commentary* on the Holy Scriptures. GEORGE BANCROFT used 26 years of his life on *History of the United States*. Sir ISAAC NEWTON seldom went to bed before 2 A.M.

In the British Museum one can see 75 drafts of THOMAS GRAY's "Elegy Written in a Country Churchyard." HEMINGWAY is said to have gone over the manuscript of "The Old Man and the Sea" 80 times.

—Selected

LOVE OF THE WHOLE PERSON

Thou shalt love the Lord thy God with all thy heart, and with all thy soul, and with all thy strength, and with all thy mind (Luke 10:27).

Duty toward God is summed up in this passage. At first sight it appears to be simple. But it requires the love of our whole being.

I. Emotional. "With all thy heart."

According to the Jews the heart is the seat of the emotions. The text emphasizes the fact that the love of God must be emotional. It need not necessarily be exuberant; it may be calm and steadfast. Many people are worried because they do not experience any sudden uprush of feeling. They need not be. Their love may be calm and gentle. The main point is that it must exist and be felt.

II. Spiritual. "With all thy soul."

This is love springing from the higher self and involves communion and union with God. It is the state of being spiritually at one with him.

III. Physical. "With all thy strength."

Strength, with the Jews, was connected with the physical body. The body must be devoted to God as the temple of the Holy Spirit. Love of Him must find expression through the body in acts of love and worship and service.

IV. Intellectual. "With all thy mind."

A wise husband studies his wife and a wise wife her husband. So, too, God must be studied. Time must be devoted to a mental consideration of His attributes, His modes of working, His means of grace, and to His holy Word. There must be an endeavor made to assimilate, mentally, to the utmost capacity of the mind, His revelation of himself.

We must love God, then, with our whole being. That love must be a true expression of our attitude toward Him.

—Selected

THREE LIFE PHILOSOPHIES

Luke 10:25–37

The Parable of the Good Samaritan presents three life philosophies:

I. That of the thieves: "Beat them up."

But the brutality of those rogues and their kind is not greater than that of the respectable manipulators who rig markets and throw great corporations into bankruptcy to line their own pockets in the name of "enlightened self-interest." One injures a man's body and steals his today; the other thrusts iron into the soul of thousands and steals their tomorrow. Our own standards are low enough to make the manipulation possible. They couldn't do it if we disliked it enough.

II. That of the priest and Levite: "Pass them up."

It had ancient if not honorable origin in the remark of a gentleman named Cain: "Am I my brother's keeper?" It gains greater acceptance when called "minding one's own business." Few of us would deliberately adopt it. Rather we drift into it as we discover one by one that our beautiful ideals are not rainbows but battles. One by one, we let our dreams go and drift into irresponsibility.

III. That of the Good Samaritan was made of brighter, cleaner stuff: "Lift them up."

Many say that it can't be done by anyone in this fast complex society. The answer is that it can be done after the manner of the Good Samaritan. Anyone who takes hold and lifts makes the whole world better. Millions have been kinder to their fellow because of that Samaritan. Good Samaritan hospitals dot the land. The lifting power of that one man staggers the imagination, and it is always so. With this philosophy, even when we fail we become the creators of the conquerors whose achievements for right we make possible by what we have valiantly attempted.

—*Paul C. Payne*